FIREFIGHTERS
to the rescue!

Bobbie Kalman

🜨 Crabtree Publishing Company

www.crabtreebooks.com

Created by Bobbie Kalman

Dedicated by Candice Murphy
To my children Adam, Emily, and Zach, who give me strength,
and to my husband Frank, my soulmate

Author and Editor-in-Chief
Bobbie Kalman

Substantive editor
Kathryn Smithyman

Project editor and research
Reagan Miller

Editors
Molly Aloian
Kristina Lundblad
Kelley MacAulay

Art director
Robert MacGregor

Design
Margaret Amy Reiach
Samantha Crabtree (series logo)

Production coordinator
Katherine Kantor

Photo research
Crystal Foxton

Consultant
Chris Leonard, Inspector, St. Catharines Fire Services

Special thanks to
Emily Murphy, Zach Murphy, Candice Murphy, Keith Makubuya, David F. Flynn and Niagara Region Children's Safety Village, Chad Bigger, Phil Duncan, and The St. Catharines Fire Department

Photographs
AP/Wide World Photos: pages 26, 27
Marc Crabtree: back cover, pages 5, 6, 7, 8 (left), 9, 10, 12-13, 16-17 (fire truck), 18, 24, 28, 29, 30, 31
© FEMA: page 23
Other images by Digital Stock and Digital Vision

Illustrations
Barbara Bedell: page 11
Margaret Amy Reiach: border, pages 10, 14, 15, 22, 30 (matches)

Crabtree Publishing Company

www.crabtreebooks.com   1-800-387-7650

Cataloging-in-Publication Data
Kalman, Bobbie.
    Firefighters to the rescue! / Bobbie Kalman.
        p. cm. -- (My community and its helpers series)
    Includes index.
    ISBN 0-7787-2096-9 (RLB) -- ISBN 0-7787-2124-8 (pbk.)
    1. Fire fighters--Juvenile literature. 2. Fire extinction--Juvenile literature. 3. Rescue work--Juvenile literature. I. Title. II. Series.
    TH9148.K3525 2004
    628.9'25--dc22
                                                2004013378
                                                    LC

Published in the United States
PMB16A
350 Fifth Ave.
Suite 3308
New York, NY
10118

Published in Canada
616 Welland Ave.,
St. Catharines, Ontario,
Canada
L2M 5V6

Published in the United Kingdom
73 Lime Walk
Headington
Oxford
OX3 7AD
United Kingdom

Published in Australia
386 Mt. Alexander Rd.,
Ascot Vale (Melbourne)
VIC 3032

Contents

What are firefighters?

Firefighters are people who fight fires. They have dangerous jobs and must be very strong and brave. Firefighters know a lot about fires. They fight fires in many places, such as buildings, cars, boats, and forests.

Community helpers

Firefighters are **community helpers**. A **community** is an area and the people who live in that area. Community helpers are people who work to keep communities safe, healthy, and fun. They also teach people how to stay safe. Doctors, police officers, and teachers are other community helpers.

Firefighters fight fires, but they also do other jobs in their communites. Keep reading to learn about other jobs firefighters do.

Rescue workers

Firefighters are also **rescue workers**. Rescue workers are people who save others from danger. Firefighters rescue people who are trapped in cars or burning houses. They also rescue people when there are **disasters**, such as floods or earthquakes.

Firefighters are teachers

Another important part of a firefighter's job is teaching people how fires can be **prevented**, or stopped from happening. There are many ways to prevent fires, which you can read about on pages 30-31.

These children are visiting a fire station to learn how firefighters keep their communities safe.

The fire station

Firefighters work at **fire stations**. A fire station is a building where firefighters store their equipment and prepare for **emergencies**. Firefighters are always ready to help people—even during the night!

While they are waiting

When there are no fires, firefighters are busy making sure they are ready for any emergency. They check their equipment and their trucks to make sure they are working properly. Firefighters also practice new firefighting skills. They need to know the best ways to fight fires!

This firefighter is checking the breathing equipment that firefighters wear inside burning buildings.

Fire stations have garages for fire trucks. The garage doors are big, and they open quickly.

Inside a fire station

There are several rooms inside a fire station. Different things happen in each room. Not all fire stations are the same, but many stations have garages and offices. The pictures below show some of the other rooms usually found in a fire station.

*The **radio room** is the room where firefighters receive information about fires. To report an emergency, people call a local emergency number, such as 911. A **dispatcher** answers the call and then contacts a firefighter in the radio room to let them know about the emergency.*

*Many fire stations have **exercise rooms**. Firefighters use exercise machines, such as **treadmills** and weight machines, to keep their bodies in good shape.*

*Some firefighters work up to 24 hours at a time. When they work for many hours, firefighters sleep in a room called a **dormitory**.*

*Firefighters prepare their meals and eat them in the **mess room**, or kitchen. They take turns cleaning the mess room after each meal.*

From head to toe

When firefighters fight fires, they are covered from head to toe in special clothing called **turnout gear**. This clothing is made from **fire-resistant** materials. Fire-resistant materials protect firefighters from the heat and flames of fires.

Great gear

A firefighter's turnout gear can be many colors, such as black, brown, or yellow. The gear has **reflective tape** on it. Reflective tape glows in the dark. It helps people see firefighters, even when they are in smoke-filled rooms.

Getting dressed

Before firefighters leave the station to fight a fire, they put on their turnout gear. Their gear is always ready so they can get dressed quickly.

This firefighter's rubber boots are already tucked inside his pants. He steps into the pants and boots at the same time.

*The pants are held up by **suspenders**. Knee pads protect the firefighter's knees when he has to crawl through a burning building.*

*The firefighter then puts on his **waterproof** jacket. Water cannot get through something that is waterproof, so the firefighter will stay dry.*

*The firefighter's gloves are made of fire-resistant leather. They fit tightly at the wrist to keep out **embers**, or small pieces of burning material.*

face shield

brim

*The firefighter wears a hard helmet to protect his head. The wide **brim** at the back of the helmet stops sparks from burning his neck. The **face shield** protects his face.*

Tools and equipment

flashlight

Firefighters use many kinds of tools and equipment to fight fires. Some basic tools are flashlights, goggles, ear protectors, and **bolt cutters**. Firefighters know when and how to use all their tools and equipment.

bolt cutters

*This firefighter is wearing a **self-contained breathing apparatus** over his face. This equipment helps him breathe when he is in a smoke-filled room. A tube inside the face mask is connected to an **air tank**. The firefighter breathes the air that flows into the mask from the air tank.*

Firefighting equipment

Some of the tools and equipment firefighters use help them rescue people trapped inside burning buildings. Other pieces of equipment help keep firefighters safe while they are fighting fires. Read on to learn more about the different types of equipment firefighters use.

*The **pick axe** is used to make holes in walls, in case someone is trapped inside a room.*

*The **Halligan tool** is used to pry open doors or windows to allow air into a room.*

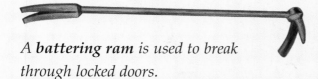

*A **battering ram** is used to break through locked doors.*

*A **saw** is used to cut through roofs and heavy doors.*

*Each firefighter wears a **personal alert safety system** (PASS) that beeps if he or she has not moved in 45 seconds. If a firefighter is injured and cannot call out, the PASS alarm will beep so the firefighter can be found.*

*A **thermal imaging device** is used to find people or animals in smoke-filled or hidden areas. This tool tracks **body heat**, or the heat that a person's or animal's body gives off.*

Fire trucks

There are many kinds of fire trucks. Most fire trucks are 30 to 50 feet (9-15 m) long. Some carry long hoses and water. Others have tall ladders.

Lights and sirens

All fire trucks have loud sirens and bright flashing lights. The lights and sirens let people know that firefighters are on their way! The lights and sounds also warn other drivers on the road to pull over, so the fire trucks can get to the fire as quickly as possible.

*Firefighters sit in the **engine cab** as they ride to a fire. They wear seat belts.*

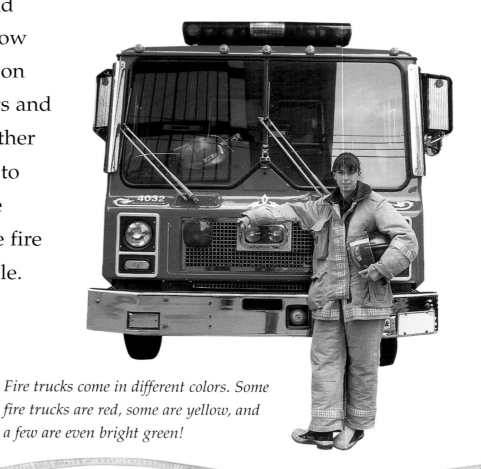

Fire trucks come in different colors. Some fire trucks are red, some are yellow, and a few are even bright green!

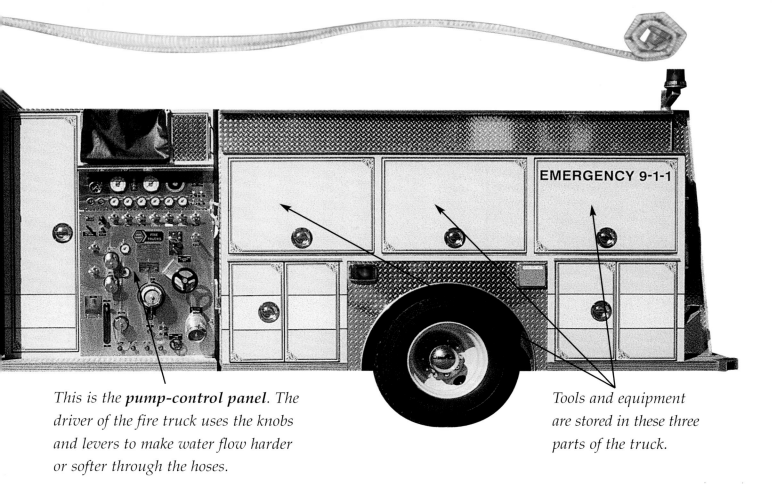

This is the **pump-control panel**. The driver of the fire truck uses the knobs and levers to make water flow harder or softer through the hoses.

Tools and equipment are stored in these three parts of the truck.

EMERGENCY 9-1-1

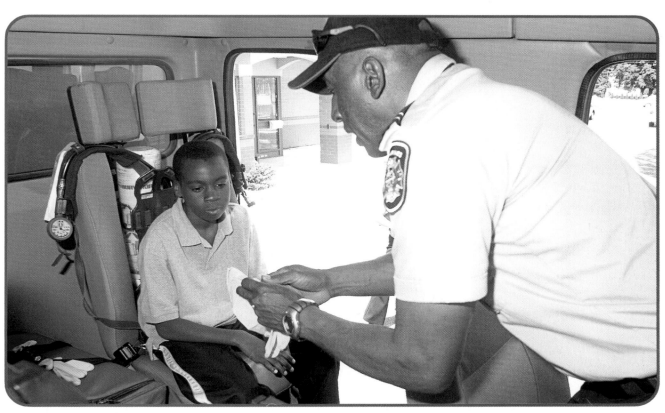

Fire trucks also carry **first-aid** supplies, such as rubber gloves and bandages.

The pumper truck

The **pumper truck** carries hoses and tools that firefighters need for fighting a fire. The firefighters who ride in the pumper truck are known as the **pumper company**. The pumper truck is usually the first truck to arrive at a fire. The pumper company finds the nearest **fire hydrant** and opens it. A fire hydrant is a covered pipe that sticks out of the ground and is connected to an underground water supply. A firefighter takes a hose that is attached to the pumper truck and connects it to the fire hydrant. The pumper truck then pumps the water from the fire hydrant into other hoses that are also connected to the pumper truck. Firefighters carry these hoses to the fire and spray water onto the flames until the fire is out.

fire hydrant

14

Working the hose

Pumps inside the pumper truck make water blast out of the hoses. The driver of the pumper truck works the control panel to make sure the water comes out hard enough to put out the fire. The water comes out so fast and hard that it can knock down a firefighter if he or she holds the hose alone.

Tiring work!

It takes at least two or three firefighters to hold a hose. One person holds the **nozzle**, shown below, while the others hold on to the hose. Holding and pointing the nozzle is very tiring work. Firefighters take turns doing this difficult job. It can take firefighters several hours to put out a big fire!

nozzle

The ladder truck

After carrying a hose up the ladder, this firefighter is aiming the water at the fire below.

Some fires are in tall buildings. Firefighters cannot put out these fires from the ground. They need to use a **ladder truck**. The ladder truck has a big ladder attached to it.

Raising the ladders

The bottom of the ladder is on a **turntable**. A turntable is a platform that turns so the ladder can face any direction. The driver of the ladder truck turns the ladder toward the fire. He or she then raises the ladder. The firefighters from the **ladder company** climb up the tall ladders to reach the fires.

At the end of some ladders, there are small metal cages called **baskets**. This firefighter is standing in a basket and shooting water down onto the flames.

Who does what?

All firefighters work hard to protect
people from fires. They have many jobs.
To make sure everything gets done,
firefighters divide up the jobs. These
pages show just a few of the jobs they do.

The fire chief

At each fire, the **fire chief** decides which jobs need to be done first. The most important job is saving lives. The fire chief keeps track of all the firefighters and makes sure they do their jobs properly.

The pumper company

Firefighters in the pumper company are often part of the **interior sector**. The interior sector is a group of firefighters who find and rescue people trapped inside burning buildings. These firefighters use thermal imaging devices to find people in dark, smoke-filled rooms.

The ladder company

Firefighters in the ladder company are often part of the **exterior sector**. The exterior sector puts out any flames that could spread to nearby buildings. They fight the flames that are behind or beside burning buildings. They also climb up ladders to put out the flames on rooftops.

Two firefighters from the pumper company are holding a hose as it sprays water onto the flames.

Firefighters use axes to break windows. Breaking windows allows gases and smoke to escape.

Rescuing people

Firefighters know how to get people out of burning buildings safely and quickly! They usually guide people out of buildings to make sure the people do not fall. Firefighters carry out young children or people who have been hurt in a fire. They help people safely climb down ladders from tall buildings.

This boy is crying because he is scared, but he will soon be safe. The firefighter is rescuing both him and his teddy bear.

Fires are scary!

Some people are so frightened by fire that they hide under beds, in closets, and in cupboards. Firefighters must search a burning building for people who might be hiding.

Medical helpers

All firefighters are trained to give first aid, but some firefighters know more about helping people who are hurt. These firefighters have taken special training courses to become **emergency medical service** (EMS) workers. EMS workers are trained to treat people with burns or people who have breathed in too much smoke. They examine people and rush those with serious injuries to nearby hospitals. EMS workers also care for other firefighters who have been injured while fighting fires or rescuing people.

EMS workers help people who have been hurt in emergencies such as fires or car accidents.

Not just fires!

Firefighters help in many kinds of emergencies. They rescue people who are trapped in cars at car crashes. Firefighters save people who are stranded in floods and people who have fallen through the ice on frozen lakes and rivers. Firefighters have equipment, including ropes and straps, to reach people who are stuck in elevators or on rooftops.

When firefighters need extra help, they use radios to call other firefighters at nearby fire stations.

At car crashes, firefighters use a tool called the **Jaws of Life** to force open car doors. When the doors are open, firefighters can pull out people who are stuck inside the cars.

9/11, a terrible day!

September 11, 2001 was a terrible day. In New York City, **terrorists** crashed two airplanes into the twin towers of the World Trade Center. Another plane crashed into the Pentagon in Virginia. A fourth airplane crashed in the countryside in Pennsylvania. All the people on the airplanes died in the crashes. Thousands of people died or were seriously injured trying to get out of the buildings that were destroyed.

The heroes

When the planes crashed into the towers, huge fires broke out and several large buildings collapsed. On that day, 343 firefighters died trying to save people's lives. These firefighters are heroes because they went into dangerous places and risked their lives to rescue others.

Thousands helped

After the disaster happened, thousands of firefighters, police officers, and other rescue workers from across the United States and Canada arrived in New York and Virginia to help. They used trained dogs, **cranes**, and other equipment to dig through the **rubble** to find and rescue people.

Firefighters used trained rescue dogs to help them find people who were trapped under the collapsed buildings.

Becoming a firefighter

Becoming a firefighter takes a lot of hard work. Firefighters have to be strong and brave. To become a firefighter, you must do well in school and enjoy subjects such as science, physical education, and English. Below is a list of skills and training you need to become a firefighter.

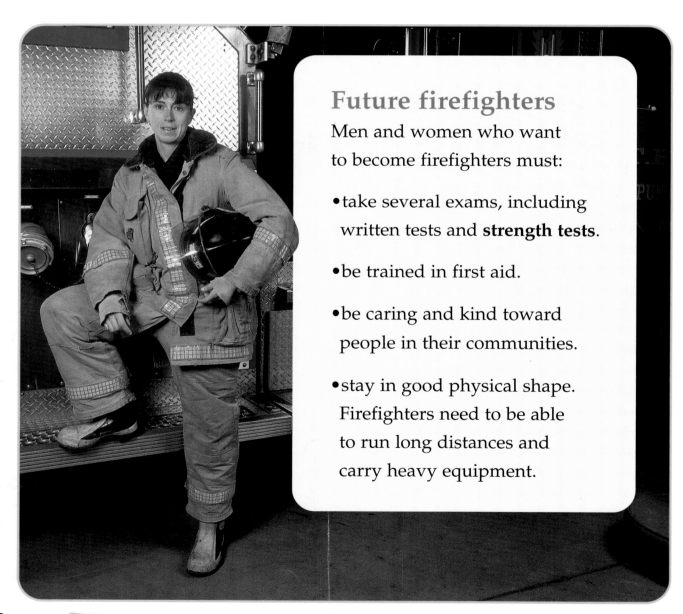

Future firefighters

Men and women who want to become firefighters must:

• take several exams, including written tests and **strength tests**.

• be trained in first aid.

• be caring and kind toward people in their communities.

• stay in good physical shape. Firefighters need to be able to run long distances and carry heavy equipment.

Helping out

You can help the firefighters in your community by teaching your family and friends about fire safety. It is important that everyone in your home or at your school knows what to do in case of a fire. Turn the page to learn some safety tips that you can teach others!

This girl is climbing down a fire ladder to practice escaping from a window in case of an emergency.

This firefighter is teaching children important safety tips that they can use to prevent fires in their homes and schools.

Fire safety

Listed below are some safety tips that you can practice with your family and friends. These tips can help save your life if a fire breaks out. In an emergency, the most important thing to remember is to stay calm and to get away from danger safely.

Make an escape plan

With your family, draw a map of your home. Plan two ways to get out of every room in case of a fire. Pick a meeting place outside your home where everyone will gather once they are out of the house. Choose one person who will call the fire department from a neighbor's house. Make sure your whole family practices the escape plan at least twice a year.

Testing, testing

Be sure that there is a working smoke alarm on each level of your home. Test the smoke alarms every month. Change their batteries twice a year.

Stop, drop, and roll!

If your clothes catch fire, do not run! Drop to the ground, cover your face with your hands, and roll on the ground. Rolling will put out the flames.

Not for kids!

Matches and lighters are tools, not toys. Never play with matches or lighters! You could start a fire without meaning to.

Down low

Smoke is very dangerous! If you are in a smoke-filled room, crawl on your hands and knees to the closest exit. If the room is so smoky that you cannot see clearly, use your hands to feel around the room and find the exit. Stay close to the floor because the air near the floor is less smoky and safer to breathe.

Take the stairs

Always use stairways to leave a building during a fire. Never use an elevator. The elevator could get stuck on a floor where the fire is burning.

Get out and stay out!

If a fire breaks out in your home or school, do not take anything with you. Leave the building as quickly and as carefully as possible.

Do not go back into a burning building for any reason! All firefighters are trained to search burning buildings. They will rescue people and pets from fires. Do not try to save anyone yourself!

Glossary

Note: Boldfaced words that are defined in the text may not appear in the glossary.

air tank A tank filled with air that pumps into an air mask

crane A large machine with long cables that is used for lifting and moving heavy objects

disaster An event that destroys parts of a community and injures people

dispatcher A person who sends out firefighters, police, or ambulances to emergencies and provides information about an emergency

emergency A serious situation that happens unexpectedly and requires immediate action

first aid Emergency medical care that is given to an injured or sick person before a doctor is available

Jaws of Life A tool with clawlike metal parts that can be put inside a damaged vehicle and spread open to free injured or trapped people

rubble The broken pieces of a building that has been destroyed

strength test A physical test that measures how strong a person is

terrorist A person who commits violent acts against people or property to force a government or community to obey his or her wishes

treadmill An exercise machine on which people can walk or run while staying in one place

Index

1 2 3 4 5 6 7 8 9 0 Printed in the U.S.A. 4 3 2 1 0 9 8 7 6 5